Thanksgiving

I've got a fun activity for you on page 22!

M. C. Hall

Little World Holidays and Celebrations

www.rourkepublishing.com

www.rourkepublishing.com

Photo credits: Courtney Weittenhiller/iStockphoto, cover; Tom Stewart/Photolibrary, 1, 4; Monkey Business/Fotolia, 3; Terrance Emerson/Shutterstock Images, 5; iStockphoto, 6; Library of Congress, 7, 9, 12, 14; SuperStock/Getty Images, 8; Rolf Fischer/iStockphoto, 10; North Wind Picture Archives/Photolibrary, 11; Jeremy Sterk/iStockphoto, 13; Ariel Skelley/Blend Images/AP Images, 15; Brian Steele/Shutterstock Images, 16; Michael Blanc/iStockphoto, 17; Andrew McDonough/Shutterstock Images, 18; Melissa Carroll/iStockphoto, 19; Alden Pellett/AP Images, 20; Bob Ingelhart/iStockphoto, 21

Editor: Holly Saari

Cover and page design: Kazuko Collins

Content Consultant: Laura M. Chmielewski, PhD, Assistant Professor of History, Purchase College, State University of New York

Library of Congress Cataloging-in-Publication Data

Hall, Margaret, 1947-
 Thanksgiving / M.C. Hall.
   p. cm. -- (Little world holidays and celebrations)
 Includes bibliographical references and index.
 ISBN 978-1-61590-239-2 (hard cover) (alk. paper)
 ISBN 978-1-61590-479-2 (soft cover)
 1. Thanksgiving Day--Juvenile literature. I. Title.
 GT4975.H36 2010
 394.2649--dc22
                                         2010009914

Rourke Publishing
Printed in the United States of America, North Mankato, Minnesota
033010
033010LP

www.rourkepublishing.com - rourke@rourkepublishing.com
Post Office Box 643328 Vero Beach, Florida 32964

What are these people doing?

They are celebrating Thanksgiving!

Each fall, farmers **harvest** their **crops**. For hundreds of years, people have had feasts to celebrate and give thanks for the food they grow.

One important harvest feast took place almost
400 years ago.

In 1620 people from England sailed to America. They came to make a new home. These **colonists** are often called **Pilgrims**.

The first winter in America was very hard. The colonists did not have enough to eat. About half of them died.

A Native American **tribe**, the Wampanoag, lived nearby. In the spring the Wampanoags helped the colonists.

The Wampanoags showed the colonists how to grow new crops, such as corn and pumpkins.

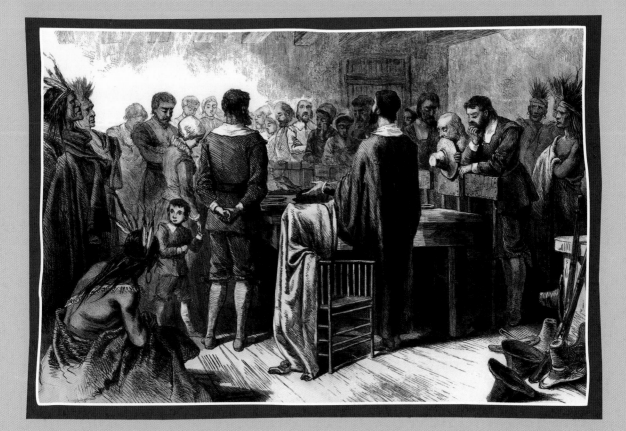

That fall the colonists had a feast to celebrate
their harvest. They asked the Wampanoags to
come.

The feast lasted for three days. Many people call this feast the first Thanksgiving.

After the first Thanksgiving, many people set aside a day to feast and give thanks each year.

President Abraham Lincoln set aside a day to give thanks in 1863. Today we celebrate Thanksgiving on the fourth Thursday in November.

Thanksgiving is a day to spend with family and friends. Many people travel a long way to be together.

Sharing a big meal is one Thanksgiving **tradition**. Many people eat turkey, stuffing, and cranberries.

Parades are another Thanksgiving tradition.
Some towns and cities have parades to
celebrate the holiday.

There is a big Thanksgiving Day parade in New York City. It has many large balloons. Millions of people watch the parade each year.

Some people go to football games on Thanksgiving Day. Many others watch games on television or play outside with friends and family.

Helping others is another Thanksgiving tradition. People give food to families that do not have enough to eat.

That way, everyone can give thanks for a good meal.

Craft: Fall Leaf Turkey

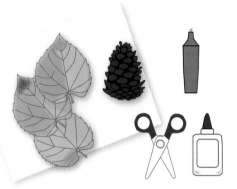

What you need:
- 10-15 fall leaves
- pinecone
- glue
- white paper
- scissors
- markers

1. Spread the leaves out on a sheet of paper. Arrange them into a fan shape going to the paper's edges. The leaves will be the turkey's feathers. Then glue the leaves onto the paper.

2. The pinecone will be the body. Place the pinecone on its side in the middle of the leaves as if the turkey is looking straight at you. Now glue the pinecone to the leaves.

3. Next make eyes and a beak for your turkey. You can draw them and cut them out of paper.

4. Glue the eyes and beak onto the pinecone body and admire your masterpiece!

Glossary

colonists (KOL-uh-nists): people who come to a new land to make a home

crops (KROPS): plants that are grown in large amounts and used for food

harvest (HAR-vist): to gather crops

Pilgrims (PIL-gruhms): the English colonists who came to America in 1620

tradition (truh-DISH-uhn): something that is done in the same way for many years

tribe (TRIBE): a group of people who share the same ancestors and customs

Websites to Visit

www.history.com/content/thanksgiving

www.plimoth.org/education/olc/index_js2.html#

www.plimoth.org/kids/

www.theholidayzone.com/thanks/printable.html

About the Author

M. C. Hall is a former elementary school teacher and an education consultant. As a freelance writer, she has authored teacher materials and more than 100 books for young readers. Hall lives and works in southeastern Massachusetts.